STAND STRONG

D1638660

60 DAYS FOR

CWR

CONTENTS

INTRO

Guys, life can be tough. Sometimes, life can be *really* tough. Not many people knew that better than the blokes in the Old Testament – but when life was tough, they got tough too. They stood up to tyrants, they faced up to famine, they trekked across deserts and climbed mountains and fought armies.

These guys were like the Expendables in sandals!

We'll look at lion-taming Daniel, Elijah's escape plan, and we'll introduce the Judges (imagine Judge Dredd but with a scroll in one hand and a sword in the other, ready to take on any opponent in the name of God).

Armour up, buckle up and fire up the TARDIS, 'cos we're going *old school*!

Enjoy the journey!

'A sword for the LORD and for Gideon!' **Judges 7:20**

DAN LIONHEART 01
EVERYTHING GOING FOR HIM

'Then the king ordered Ashpenaz, chief of his court officials, to bring into the king's service some of the Israelites from the royal family and the nobility – young men without any physical defect, handsome, showing aptitude for every kind of learning, well informed, quick to understand, and qualified to serve in the king's palace.' **Daniel 1:3–4**

Daniel was a young lad with everything going for him. Sadly, one of those going for him was King Nebuchadnezzar. This ***POWERFUL KING*** of the mighty Babylonian Empire cruised into Jerusalem and flattened the city (just as God had warned). The Jewish survivors, including Daniel, were rounded up and taken back to Babylon as slaves.

Daniel and a few of his high-flying mates were spared the hard labour camps and put on a three-year training course to become apprentice wise men.

This must have been a really unsettling experience for Daniel. The chances of ever seeing his homeland again were very slim! So what would he do now? Did God still care about him? **DID HE STILL CARE ABOUT GOD?**

>ENGAGE

Major changes in our lives can sometimes cause us to question our faith. If those changes unsettle or upset us we may think God is giving us a bad time. Daniel didn't react like that. He trusted that the God he worshipped in Jerusalem would look after him in Babylon. And he kept talking with God three times a day throughout the whole crisis. Now that sounds sensible!

PRAY

Lord, when changes or challenges shake my faith, help me to remember to trust You, not blame You. Amen.

TRUST

FIVE STAR SERVICE

'But Daniel resolved not to defile himself with the royal food and wine, and he asked the chief official for permission not to defile himself in this way. Now God had caused the official to show favour and compassion to Daniel, but the official told Daniel, "I am afraid of my lord the king, who has assigned your food and drink. Why should he see you looking worse than the other young men of your age? The king would then have my head because of you."' **Daniel 1:8–10**

So what was all the fuss about the menu?

Daniel, the **FOREIGN SLAVE,** was being served up the best food and drink in the land! The problem was that the five-star food wasn't recommended by God because it had been **OFFERED TO IDOLS** before being served to Daniel.

Who cares?

No one was watching. No one would find out. Complaining would mean a one-way trip to the lions' den. But Daniel cared! If it was wrong, it was wrong no matter where you were or who you were with. And **BECAUSE DANIEL CARED, HE DARED!**

He decided to start out the way he meant to carry on – by doing things God's way.

He didn't launch into a sermon about the evils of Babylonian junk food. That would have got right up the Babylonian noses. Instead, he suggested that he swapped his food with the servants. Now they didn't complain about that! Their only worry was whether Daniel and his Jewish friends would end up looking all skin and bone, which would have led to questions being asked.

Here Dan discovered that if you put God first, He'll honour you. Instead of looking thin and gaunt, the voluntary vegetarians were brimming with health and vitality. Not only that, they graduated from their three-year course with top marks, way ahead of their wining and dining colleagues.

Daniel made up his mind to put God first in everything. Are you prepared to do the same? Talk with God about the pressures that make it tough to say and do the right thing. Ask God to help you put Him first.

DREAM ON

'The astrologers answered the king, "There is no one on earth who can do what the king asks! No king, however great and mighty, has ever asked such a thing of any magician or enchanter or astrologer. What the king asks is too difficult. No one can reveal it to the king except the gods, and they do not live among humans."' **Daniel 2:10–11**

The fortune-tellers of Babylon were mystified.

A recent archaeological find of some dream interpretation writings found in Old Babylon can help us understand why they panicked. The so-called 'wise men' recorded dreams and then observed what happened next. For example, if someone dreamt about a bunch of grapes and the next day he fell down the stairs, dreaming of grapes became a bad omen. So with a bit of huff, bluff and some sorcery thrown in, they would charge money to work out what your dreams meant.

What threw them here was that the king wouldn't, or couldn't, tell them the dream in the first place. So they were well and truly caught out. *NONE OF THEM HAD A CLUE,* including Daniel and his veggie friends who were called in to help. 'Dream on,' the Babylonian wise guys replied. 'How can we possibly know what you dreamt?'

The king was not a happy man.

He wasn't to know that it was God who had given him the troubling dream. So he decided to axe all his wise men – including Dan.

>ENGAGE

Astrologers, card readers and the like still try to tell the future from the position of the stars or the tea leaves in your cup. While some of this may appear to be harmless fun, some forms of prediction are linked to the occult. So it's always best to say no to 'having your fortune told' or messing with games like Ouija boards. There is only one Person who knows the truth, the whole truth and nothing but the truth about the future – Almighty God. So leave the future to Him, which is what Dan dared to do!

PRAY

Father God, please give me strength to not mess with fortune telling. Please help me to trust completely that you have tomorrow covered. Amen.

'When Arioch, the commander of the king's guard, had gone out to put to death the wise men of Babylon, Daniel spoke to him with wisdom and tact. He asked the king's officer, "Why did the king issue such a harsh decree?" Arioch then explained the matter to Daniel. At this, Daniel went in to the king and asked for time, so that he might interpret the dream for him.' **Daniel 2:14–16**

Just marvel at how Dan dared to handle the situation. He wasn't one to grovel and create a scene by pleading for his life. Nor did he complain at the harsh sentence. And let's face it, death is just a little 'OTT' for not knowing a dream.

Dan remained super cool. Why? He knew that he and his veggie friends had **ONE BIG CHANCE** – God. So he politely asked for a stay of execution so he could ask the God of heaven to explain the mystery.

An emergency prayer meeting was called at Dan's house. He and his friends got down to some serious talking with God, asking Him to let them in on the secret dream. Time was running out!

Later in the prayer meeting, God told Daniel the dream that had got the King of Babylon troubled. That was the end of the prayer meeting and the beginning of the praise meeting. Dan **LIFTED HIS PRAISE** into overdrive, thanking God for His power and wisdom. More than that – thanking God for sharing His wisdom with him.

>ENGAGE

If you're ever unsure of what to do about anything, talk the matter through with God. That sounds obvious for a Christian to do. But is it? Often we like to sort things out our way and only talk with God if things reach a crisis. Get into the habit of talking through the small details of your life with God. A prayer meeting in Dan's house wasn't the exception but the rule – three times a day.

PRAY

Lord, whatever comes my way, help me to keep my head and talk to You. Thank You that You're interested in even the small details of my life. Amen.

DAN LIONHEART 01

'This is the meaning of the vision of the rock cut out of a mountain, but not by human hands – a rock that broke the iron, the bronze, the clay, the silver and the gold to pieces. The great God has shown the king what will take place in the future. The dream is true and its interpretation is trustworthy.' **Daniel 2:45**

A bit of background will reveal just how daring Dan got with the king.

The Babylonians believed in lots of gods. So they didn't dismiss Dan's God, it's just that they put Him alongside the others. They did, however, believe that one god, Bel-Marduk, was the god of the gods. And, **CRAZY** as it might seem, once a year they wheeled out all the statues of the other gods to worship a huge statue of Bel-Marduk.

Daniel dared to tell the king that it was his God who was the wisest God. The God of heaven was the only One to come up with the king's dream. A fact the king couldn't deny.

Daniel also dared to say that God was the ultimate power. He explained that the materials in the statue represented the Babylonian Empire and kingdoms to come. But the ultimate kingdom would be God's kingdom – **TOTALLY UNBEATABLE.**

All the other kingdoms would end but God's kingdom would go on forever.

Daniel also dared to mention that his God was the greatest! Who had shown the king the meaning of his dream? Not Bel-Marduk, but God.

Daniel spoke humbly and powerfully. Not only did he save his friends from the death sentence but he asked the king to spare the wining and dining brigade as well. Did he take any of the credit? No, all the credit went to God. He didn't claim to be smarter than any of the other wise guys, it was just that his God is alive.

Have you ever dared to give God the credit for helping you in front of others? Why not ask for a bit of help? With God's help you can!

Father, thank You for all you do in my life. Please help me have the voice to credit You to other poeple. Amen.

FINAL BOSS

'The king said to Daniel, "Surely your God is the God of gods and the Lord of kings and a revealer of mysteries, for you were able to reveal this mystery." Then the king placed Daniel in a high position and lavished many gifts on him. He made him ruler over the entire province of Babylon and placed him in charge of all its wise men.' **Daniel 2:47–48**

This is unreal! The king of the *MOST POWERFUL KINGDOM* on earth is grovelling before Daniel. The king is awed by God's power: 'God is the God of gods! God is the Lord of kings!' Bel-Marduk is history.

One day every king who has ever governed and every big cheese who has ever led, will bow and declare that Jesus is King of kings and Lord of lords. Yes, the president of the USA, Richard Branson, the Sultan of Brunei – you name them – one day will over-awed into saying who the real *BIG BOSS* is. And so will you!

For Daniel this was a dream come true!

Not only did he get to keep his head but also he was promoted to be in charge of the province of Babylon. His friends were promoted too. Those who dare to put God first are honoured in return.

So what was the first thing Daniel did after getting his new job? Why, pray of course. He did that three times a day! He wasn't one to pass up an opportunity to talk with the King of kings and Lord of lords.

>ENGAGE

God puts people in their place. The mighty king went down and humble Dan went up! Why not get down to some King of kings-sized praising? He's totally worthy of it!

PRAY

God, You are amazing. Thank You for being greater than any other and best of all for being by my side. Amen.

AMAZING

STAND UP

'But there are some Jews whom you have set over the affairs of the province of Babylon – Shadrach, Meshach and Abednego – who pay no attention to you, Your Majesty. They neither serve your gods nor worship the image of gold you have set up.' **Daniel 3:12**

Three of Daniel's Jewish prayer partners were in the hot seat.

They'd been promoted with Daniel to top jobs, which didn't go down too well with the Babylonian born and bred yuppies. When Nebuchadnezzar built a huge golden idol (the dream about him being a 'head of gold' had inflated his ego – see 2:31–33, 36–38), the anti-Jewish lobby got their chance to get Meshach, Shadrach and Abednego fired.

The three lads were put in a difficult situation.

They could either **KEEP THEIR HEADS DOWN** and go along with the crowd, or **STAND UP** for what they believed. In the past they'd followed Daniel's example and refused to eat forbidden food. They had prayed with Daniel and seen God answer their prayers. Now what? Daniel wasn't there to help them this time.

18

The lads knew that God had put them in influential jobs to be an example to all the other captured Jews slaving away in Babylon. If they grovelled to idols then God's name would be dishonoured. It was vital they remained loyal to God while they waited for Him to rescue them and return them to Israel.

When the band played, the lads didn't move (3:10–12). Nor did they compromise in any way to avoid being fried. They stood for God and faced the music.

>ENGAGE

When 'everyone else is doing it' and what they are doing is wrong, how do you react? It can be really hard to say 'no' when you know others will think you're being a wimp. Daniel's friends decided to let God call the tune in their lives and not bow to pressure. When you're squeezed by others to go off limits, talk to God and ask Him to help you do the right thing. Saying 'no' may be hard at the time but it's always the best route for you in the end.

PRAY

Father God, help me to do what's right, however hard it is. When I really should say 'no', please help me to do that. Amen.

THE HEAT IS ON

'Nebuchadnezzar then approached the opening of the blazing furnace and shouted, "Shadrach, Meshach and Abednego, servants of the Most High God, come out! Come here!" So Shadrach, Meshach and Abednego came out of the fire, and the satraps, prefects, governors and royal advisors crowded around them. They saw that the fire had not harmed their bodies, nor was a hair of their heads singed; their robes were not scorched, and there was no smell of fire on them.' **Daniel 3:26–27**

The first time the band played, the lads quietly opted out of doing what everyone else was doing. God had forbidden His people to worship idols so they let the crowd lick the sand while they stood.

Nebuchadnezzar flipped his lid and gave them a grilling. All eyes were beaming in on the lads to see what they would do. This time they were under ***REAL HEAVY PRESSURE*** to follow the crowd.

The lads remained amazingly cool. Why? This wasn't their problem; it was God's problem. They calmly explained to the seriously angry king that they were going to play by God's rules. ***GOD HAD***

THE POWER to rescue them and even if He chose not to, it was better to be on fire for God than to step out of line with Him.

Even as they faced the horror of a blazing furnace they didn't backtrack on their decision. And where was God when they needed Him? Right in the heat with them. God stands by those who stand for Him.

Nebuchadnezzar, who began the day demanding praise for himself, was scorched into praising the Most High God! The three lads were promoted again. You've heard it before … God honours those who honour Him.

>**ENGAGE**

What did the lads stand to lose by saying 'no'? What did they gain? Sometimes we think that saying 'no' means missing out. It's not missing out, it's a chance to be better off. So if you are under pressure to bow out of what's right, think about the consequences. Remember that when the heat is on, God is right in there with you. Talk with Him about it.

PRESSURE

SIGNS AND WONDERS

'It is my pleasure to tell you about the miraculous signs and wonders that the Most High God has performed for me. How great are his signs, how mighty his wonders! His kingdom is an eternal kingdom; his dominion endures from generation to generation.' **Daniel 4:2–3**

Nebuchadnezzar has been dreaming on his king-sized bed again. And he knows the best person to explain the dream – Dan.

The king's words about God are very complimentary but totally mixed up.

On one hand the king thinks *GOD IS GREAT,* and holy, the most high of all the gods. He's impressed with the signs and wonders God has performed. But Nebuchadnezzar won't accept there is only *ONE TRUE GOD* and is hedging his bets by worshipping other gods as well. He's even named Dan after his favourite god, Belteshazzar.

The king's other big problem is that he thinks he's a bit of a god himself and expects to be worshipped. And it was while he was basking in self-glory, 'contented and prosperous' (4:4), that God shook him up with another puzzling dream.

Once again the so-called fortune-tellers, astrologers and occult-odd-boys couldn't understand what God was saying. Daniel was the only one who knew what God was showing the king. Why? Daniel consulted God. All the others consulted spirits that were far from holy – evil spirits. Daniel had the help of the Holy Spirit to come up with the truth.

Nebuchadnezzar is about to learn he's not a god but an absolute head case.

Dan was different. It wasn't his good looks, brains or his diplomacy that made him stand out. The difference was that Dan was in touch with the One true holy God. Daniel didn't need to look to the New Age quacks of his time for help of any kind. His God had all the answers.

 Remember that the Spirit of God living in Christians is holy. Ask God to fill you with His Spirit so you can live wholly for Him today.

CHANGE OF WAYS

'This is the interpretation ... you will be driven away from people and will live with the wild animals ... Therefore, Your Majesty, be pleased to accept my advice: renounce your sins by doing what is right, and your wickedness by being kind to the oppressed. It may be that then your prosperity will continue.' **Daniel 4:24–25,27**

How do you tell Mr Big of Babylon that God is going to take away his marbles for seven years? The proud king is heading for a complete mental breakdown.

Dan dared to tell the truth – as politely and tactfully as possible. The good news was that the big tree in the dream was none other than Nebuchadnezzer – strong and powerful. The bad news was that God was going to bring Neb and his kingdom down to earth. The king would totally flip, think he was an animal and chew the cud.

God had a method in this madness. He was giving Neb seven years to chew over the question, 'Who's the greatest?' – Neb or the Most High God? And when Neb came to his senses and credited God as the top Ruler, God would give him his kingdom back.

Dan also dared to tell the proud king the **HARD FACTS** of salvation. Neb needed to **ADMIT HE WAS WRONG** and start living God's way. That meant putting a stop to exploiting people and helping them instead.

The king listened to Dan but gave him the brush off. There was no way he was going to mend his ways or get soft on the poor. This allowed God no other option but to take action.

It takes a lot of courage to explain to someone that they're out of line with God. Would you dare say that the only escape is for them to confess their sin and trust in Jesus? What if they go quiet on you? Dan felt terrified but took a deep breath and carried on talking, because he knew it was the truth that would set the king free. Do you get into a sweat at the thought of talking with someone about Jesus? Remember that you're doing them a great favour, even if they don't realise it at the time.

CUT DOWN TO SIZE

'Now I, Nebuchadnezzar, praise and exalt and glorify the King of heaven, because everything he does is right and all his ways are just. And those who walk in pride he is able to humble.' **Daniel 4:37**

Neb totally ignored Dan's advice to get right with God. A year later, as he was still strutting and boasting about being the greatest, God *CUT HIM DOWN TO SIZE.*

The king was driven out of office, completely flipped his lid and *FREAKED OUT.* He went absolutely bonkers! But the king's real madness had been to ignore God in the first place. Mr Big of Babylon was about to learn the hard way.

It took seven years face down in the grass before proud Neb looked up to God as the boss.

The once proud king was utterly humbled. His sanity returned and he praised the Most High. And what a first rate tribute to God he wrote in his letter – the King of heaven is Number One, unquestionably the best and always right.

Neb finally did what Dan had advised him to do seven years earlier – be humble, own up and get right with God. And what a difference it made when Neb obeyed God. He was welcomed back into office and his kingdom became more powerful than ever. Guess why?

>ENGAGE

Dan dared to speak the truth to Neb but it didn't sink in for another seven years. Sometimes those you talk to about Jesus don't become Christians right away. It often takes time for people to see the sense in trusting Jesus. So ask God to help you chat freely about your faith. You never know what might happen later.

PRAY

Lord Jesus, I want to talk to other people about You. Please give me opportunities to do that, and the right words to say. Amen.

RISE UP OTHNIEL//EHUD//DEBORAH
FREE RADICAL

'The anger of the LORD burned against Israel so that he sold them into the hands of Cushan-Rishathaim king of Aram Naharaim, to whom the Israelites were subject for eight years. But when they cried out to the LORD, he raised up for them a deliverer, Othniel ... who saved them.' **Judges 3:8–9**

Way back in the Old Testament, the Israelites had a roller coaster relationship with God – up one moment, down the next. The eventful book of Judges sees the Israelites experience these highs and lows:

- They love and worship God.
- They forget God and worship false gods.
- God takes away their freedom to punish them.
- They cry out to God for help.
- God sends one of the judges to rescue them.
- The judge wins against all the odds.
- They love and worship God.

In today's reading we see the Israelites are **OPPRESSED** and **DOWN-TRODDEN** by the power of a heartless government. Although their leaders envisioned a promised land flowing with milk and honey, the ordinary bods soon find the milk's gone off and life's more like sour vinegar than sweet honey.

But eventually some brave radical who can't be silenced steps onto the scene. Enough is enough! The cry rings out for revolution.

The people, who desperately needed a deliverer, are given Othniel to help them turn their society upside down (or should that be right-side up?).

>ENGAGE

Without a leader like one of the judges, the people were sunk! For us, God has sent the ultimate leader, Jesus, the Son of God! We don't have to keep going back and forth to God, then away from Him. Not only does Jesus free us from sin, but He sends the Holy Spirit to live in us and actually changes us from the inside out!

PRAY

Father, thank You for sending Jesus and Your Holy Spirit so that I can be in constant contact with You. Help me to use that personal relationship to talk to You more. Amen.

LEADERSHIP POTENTIAL

'The Spirit of the LORD came on him, so that he became Israel's judge and went to war. The LORD gave Cushan-Rishathaim king of Aram into the hands of Othniel, who overpowered him.' **Judges 3:10**

When Othniel led his men into battle he was not hoping for a medal, but a kiss. Seriously ...

Caleb ran a rather unusual dating agency. Win the battle, win a wife. Othniel rose to the challenge and charged into the Canaanites so he could marry Caleb's daughter, Acsah. But Othniel had very little else going for him. He had to ask his bride to talk her father into giving them fertile land so they could afford to live. Othniel fades into insignificance until the Israelites jump on their roller coaster ... forgetting God ... worshipping idols ... freedom taken away by the Mesopotamians (sounds like some kind of bacteria) ... crying for help ... And the man God chose to **RESCUE THEM** was Othniel. But why is Othniel prepared to **LEAD THEM INTO BATTLE?**

There isn't a good-looking prize on offer. The answer is that God gave His Spirit to Othniel and made him into a powerful, courageous leader. Not only did God help Othniel win the battle but also to rule in peacetime.

>ENGAGE

We don't become more powerful Christians by eating fitness foods and working out to keep-fit DVDs. In our daily battle to live as God wants, we need the Holy Spirit to fire us into action. Talk with God about the struggles you sometimes have in doing things His way and ask for Holy Spirit power to help you defeat harmful habits.

PRAY

Father, remind me to ask You for help, through Your Holy Spirit, to live for You. Amen.

CLOAK AND DAGGER

'Again the Israelites cried out to the LORD, and he gave them a deliverer – Ehud … The Israelites sent him … to Eglon king of Moab … Ehud then approached him while he was sitting alone in the upper room of his palace and said, "I have a message from God for you." As the king rose from his seat, Ehud reached with his left hand, drew the sword from his right thigh and plunged it into the king's belly.'

Judges 3:15,20–21

The Israelites had been roller coaster joyriding again … worshipping idols … **LOSING THEIR FREEDOM** to the Moabites … begging God to rescue them. Enter secret agent Ehud, **LICENSED TO KILL.**

SECRET AGENT PROFILE

Name: Ehud (no seriously, that's his real name).

Distinguishing features: Left-handed.

Mission: To assassinate Eglon, king of the Moabites, and then attack his army.

Weapons: 50cm dagger concealed in his cloak.

Ehud was a smooth operator. He suavely arranged a private meeting with cruel tyrannical King Eglon – the very man who had treated the Jews badly for eighteen years!

Ehud plunged in with a piercing message from God that the overweight king could not stomach. Then Ehud, not a hair out of place, quietly locked the king in the loo and calmly escaped from enemy headquarters. The first part of his mission was accomplished.

>ENGAGE

Ehud's two-sided sword certainly did the damage (and we're not spared the gory details). God says that His Word is like a two-edged sword. Have you ever experienced how the Bible stabs at our consciences and helps us to discover what is right and wrong? If you know there is something you need to put right, talk it through with God now.

FOLLOW ME

'"Follow me," he ordered, "for the LORD has given Moab, your enemy, into your hands." So they followed him down and took possession of the fords of the Jordan that led to Moab; they allowed no one to cross over. At that time they struck down about ten thousand Moabites, all vigorous and strong; not one escaped.

Judges 3:28–29

Ehud had assassinated the enemy king and escaped. Why are the Moabites not retaliating? They think their king is otherwise engaged ... (and they are getting desperate!).

While Ehud made his escape, the unsuspecting enemy thought their king was locked in the loo (v24)! By the time the penny had dropped, it was too late. Ehud had rallied the Israelites and was leading them into battle. **SPURRED ON** by the belief that God had already given them **VICTORY,** Ehud and his troops flushed the mighty Moabites out of the land. The Israelites put God first and enjoyed eighty years of peace.

>ENGAGE

Each time the Israelites came to God for forgiveness, He gave them back their freedom. And while they obeyed Him they lived in peace. You would have thought they'd have learnt their lesson by now. But who are we to judge? How many times have we chosen to do it our way, knowing it might cause trouble to ourselves and others? Stop and think about all the things you do. Is there anything you know you should stop, or even start? Talk with God about the temptations that are hardest to resist and ask for His help in breaking bad habits.

PRAY

Lord, thank You that I can be completely honest with You and talk to You about anything. Please reveal to me any areas of my life that I may need to change to follow You wholly. Amen.

LEARNING FROM MISTAKES

'Again the Israelites did evil in the eyes of the LORD, now that Ehud was dead. So the LORD sold them into the hands of Jabin king of Canaan, who reigned in Hazor. Sisera, the commander of his army, was based in Harosheth Haggoyim. Because he had nine hundred chariots fitted with iron and had cruelly oppressed the Israelites for twenty years, they cried to the LORD for help.' **Judges 4:1–3**

▶ While Ehud, the **DARING LEFT-HANDED ASSASSIN,** was leading them, the Israelites lived by God's rules. Then Ehud died. Surely the Israelites would not be so foolish as to head away from God again …

The Israelites hadn't learnt from their mistakes. Without Ehud to stop them they jumped on the roller coaster and went on a screaming loop the loop away from God. They left the peace that God had brought to them and spiralled into twenty years of misery. The Canaanites, with their armoured corp of 900 chariots, tanked in to bully the Israelites mercilessly. Why are the Israelites such a bunch of fools? Why do they keep getting into trouble? Judges 2:10 gives us a clue. The new generation, who had grown up when times were good, did not put their **TRUST IN GOD.**

>ENGAGE

Each and every person becomes a child of God by trusting Him for themselves. This act of trusting is something God helps us to do; Jesus calls it being 'born again'. After being born into your family, you need to be 'born again' into God's family. How do you know if this has happened? Well, if you are starting to think about God and how He might think or act in situations, you are probably experiencing His Holy Spirit at work. If you know that you want to live for God and tell other people about Him, go for it, as you are part of His family and He wants to help you.

PRAY

Father, help me to listen to You and give me courage to do what I hear You asking me to. Amen.

STUCK IN THE MUD

'Deborah, a prophet ... sent for Barak ... and said to him, "The LORD, the God of Israel, commands you: 'Go, take with you ten thousand men of Naphtali and Zebulun and lead them up to Mount Tabor. I will lead Sisera, the commander of Jabin's army, with his chariots and his troops to the River Kishon and give him into your hands.'" Barak said to her, "If you go with me, I will go; but if you don't go with me, I won't go." "Certainly I will go with you," said Deborah. "But because of the course you are taking, the honour will not be yours, for the LORD will deliver Sisera into the hands of a woman."'

Judges 4:4, 6–9

The Israelites had been pushed around for twenty years by the heavily armed Canaanites. And there was not a man brave enough to take them on. But Deborah was not a man.

Deborah **WASN'T SCARED** of the Canaanites. She was a prophetess, filled with the Holy Spirit. God had told her that He was going to defeat the enemy, and she believed Him. Barak would only lead the Israelite troops if Deborah was there to hold his hand.

So brave Deborah **RALLIED THE TROOPS** and sent them on a charge down the mountain towards 900 heavily armed chariots. The two-wheel drive enemy chariots couldn't cope with the boggy conditions in the flooded river valley. As the Canaanites got stuck in the mud, the Israelites got stuck in. Spurred on by Deborah, the Israelites won a famous victory. God can do mighty things through those who trust Him – male or female.

>ENGAGE

God gives His power to both guys and girls. Deborah was the only person prepared to act on God's command and God backed her all the way. God wants you to be part of His plans – don't wimp out when He wants you to do something for Him. And don't make the mistake of thinking girls are the 'fairer sex'; treat everyone equally, whether they're male or female.

PRAY

Dear God, thank You for making us all unique and for treating us all equally. May I always remember that we are all part of Your family and that You love us all the same. Amen.

RELUCTANT HERO

'Ahab son of Omri became king of Israel, and he ... did more evil in the eyes of the LORD than any of those before him ... Now Elijah the Tishbite, from Tishbe in Gilead, said to Ahab, "As the LORD, the God of Israel, lives, whom I serve, there will be neither dew nor rain in the next few years except at my word."'

1 Kings 16:29–30; 17:1

King Ahab made a lot of big mistakes, including his choice of wife. Jezebel was a pushy woman who influenced him to worship Baal and goddess Asherah. Consequently the altars of God were torn down and replaced with altars to Baal.

Then along came Elijah, our **RELUCTANT HERO** – a wild man kitted out in camel hair who championed God's cause against all the odds. His name means 'Yahweh is God' and that's what he believed. Elijah thought he was the only man in the land who still worshipped God. He was wrong. There were 7,000 Jews loyal to God, but they were keeping quiet about it to save their skins.

So what did Elijah do when God told him to get into Ahab's ivory towers with a message? He didn't bottle out or use email. He squared up to Ahab.

His message was a direct challenge to Baal, whom Ahab worshipped as the god who sent rain. God was going to show who was boss by turning off the rain and dew (for three and a half years, as it turned out).

>ENGAGE

Why was Elijah prepared to speak up for God when 7,000 others stayed quiet? Elijah had the Spirit of God on him. The Holy Spirit turns cold into bold.

PRAY

Lord, thank You that You understand my fears and can help me overcome them. Help me to be bold and strong. Amen.

THROW DOWN

'Then the word of the LORD came to Elijah: "Leave here, turn eastward and hide in the Kerith Ravine, east of the Jordan. You will drink from the brook, and I have instructed the ravens to supply you with food there." So he did what the LORD had told him.' **1 Kings 17:2–5**

Elijah had left the security of his home town of Tishbe in Gilead to become God's spokesman. Having **THROWN DOWN THE GAUNTLET** to Ahab – no dew for the Jews – it looks as though Elijah needs to make his exit from Samaria.

But where now? God had an **ESCAPE PLAN** for His brave prophet, but He didn't explain it until Elijah had carried out the first part of the mission.

> **GOD'S ESCAPE PLAN 1:** Head east, young man. Cross the Jordan and hide in the desert in the Kerith Ravine. A squadron of ravens will fly in supplies to you each day.

Hang on a minute. When the water is going to be switched off it doesn't make sense to head into the desert. And as for the food supply – it sounds ravin' mad.

Ravens are selfish birds of prey. They don't share their food, they snatch it. So is Elijah going to go along with this bird-brained scheme?

Yes! He 'did what the Lord had told him' and camped out in the dropping zone. God turned the plunderbirds into wonderbirds (He has the ability to change us too). Twice a day the ravens came in low to supply the needs of God's man.

>ENGAGE

Elijah went where God wanted him to and got dive-bombed with food. Had he gone elsewhere he might well have starved. When we do what God asks, His power is released to take care of our personal needs. It may seem mad to do what God wants at times, but it's always for our good.

PRAY

Lord, please help me to trust that You always want what's best for me. Amen.

UP THE CREEK

'Some time later the brook dried up because there had been no rain in the land. Then the word of the LORD came to him: "Go at once to Zarephath in the region of Sidon and stay there. I have instructed a widow there to supply you with food."' **1 Kings 17:7–9**

Elijah is up the creek, but not without food. At dawn and dusk (preying times for ravens; praying times for Elijah) the food lands in his lap. Water is on tap from the small brook but supplies are drying up.

Was Elijah getting a little scared watching his water supply dwindle to a trickle and then dry up altogether? The situation would only get worse as the drought continued. What would happen to him now? He was a wanted man, but still Elijah stayed put until God told him to move. And God had another escape plan mapped out.

> ## GOD'S ESCAPE PLAN 2: Go to the seaport of Zarephath in Sidon. I have arranged for a widow to feed you.

Is this crazy or what? Sidon is where Jezebel came from – a Baal-worshipping nation. And what help will a widow be? Widows rarely have enough food to eat.

Elijah didn't find this a problem. God who had **SUPPLIED HIS NEEDS** in a desert ravine would look after him in Sidon. The important thing was to be where God wanted – doing what God wanted.

>ENGAGE

Sometimes when circumstances change, our lives change too. Money, like brooks, can dry up. Hopes can disappear as exam results arrive. You may have to move to a new area or school. How do you cope with change? Elijah didn't fear the future, he knew God had already worked it out. If ever things fall apart around you – fall heavily on God. He works all things 'for the good of those who love him' (Rom. 8:28).

CHANGE

SCRAPING THE BARREL

'For this is what the LORD, the God of Israel, says: "The jar of flour will not be used up and the jug of oil will not run dry until the day the LORD sends rain on the land."' **1 Kings 17:14**

Elijah knows that God has arranged for a widow to feed him. What he doesn't know is that the widow is preparing her last meal … until he arrives in Zarephath.

The widow and her son expect to die of starvation, but Elijah is expecting to be fed by them. **WHAT'S GONE WRONG?** Nothing! God tells Elijah that He will keep topping up the widow's flour and oil during the drought. God's promise is enough for Elijah, but how will the widow react?

The widow was a Sidonian – from the capital city of Baal worship. Why should she trust the God of Israel? We don't know why she pinned her last hopes on God, but she did. And to prove it she shared her 'last' meal with Elijah.

And **GOD KEPT HIS PROMISE.** The flour jar that had been emptied kept refilling each time it was used, as did the jug of oil (for over three years)! When God's around there's no need to scrape the barrel.

The widow had given flour and oil to God to feed Elijah, and God replied by giving her all she, her family and Elijah needed. When you trust in God, you may be surprised at the ways in which He will give to you.

>ENGAGE

By being in the right place at the right time Elijah introduced a woman and her family to the living God. It saved their lives. Sometimes we don't let others know about the God who can save them because we don't think they'll go for it. Elijah spoke up for the Lord his God in a foreign land because he knew God had the power to change lives and situations.

PRAY

Lord, please help me to tell other people about You. Please help me to take the chances You give me to share Your truth. Amen.

WHEN DISASTER STRIKES

'The LORD heard Elijah's cry, and the boy's life returned to him, and he lived. Elijah picked up the child and carried him down from the room into the house. He gave him to his mother and said, "Look, your son is alive!"' **1 Kings 17:22–23**

Just when things are going well for the widow, **TOTAL DISASTER** strikes. Her son becomes ill and dies. 'Why has God allowed this to happen?' she cries. Have you ever asked that question too?

Troubles, sickness and difficulties are sometimes like buses: there are none for ages then three arrive at once. And when we face **TOUGH TIMES** the tendency is to think that God is punishing us for something we've done wrong. The woman wrongly thought this tragedy was God's way of reminding her of her past failures.

Elijah cared, and cared enough to do the only thing he could – pray. He shared the mother's distress and prayed not once, or twice, but three times for the boy. Asking God to bring the boy back to life was a daring thing to do, but Elijah knew that God is 'able to do immeasurably more than all we ask or imagine' (Eph. 3:20).

God powered in to answer Elijah's prayer. Any doubts the widow had about God, or fears about her past, were dispelled. God did care and had the power to show it!

>ENGAGE

When things go wrong, it's tempting to think that God doesn't care about you. Often problems aren't our fault but are the result of living in a world that's off the rails and heading away from God. What's the best thing to do in a situation that seems so unfair? Do what Elijah did and talk the matter through with God. Tell Him how you feel. He'll understand and He also has the power to do something about it.

ONE FALSE MOVE

'Now the famine was severe in Samaria, and Ahab had summoned Obadiah, his palace administrator. (Obadiah was a devout believer in the LORD. While Jezebel was killing off the LORD's prophets, Obadiah had taken a hundred prophets and hidden them in two caves, fifty in each, and had supplied them with food and water.)' **1 Kings 18:2–4**

A seal dating from this period reads, 'To Obadiah, servant of the king'. Obadiah had a top job working for King Ahab, but he didn't go along with his master's idol worship. His name means 'servant of God', and he lived up to his name.

Obadiah was a key member of God's underground movement – working undercover in enemy head-quarters. When Jezebel gave orders for God's prophets to be executed, Obadiah hid 100 of them in two caves and smuggled food and water to them (probably from the palace larders). 'Obadiah was a devout believer' and ***PROVED IT BY HIS ACTIONS.*** One false move would have cost him his life.

Two years of Baal worship hadn't produced a drop of rain and the situation was getting desperate. Ahab was mad with Elijah and gunning for him, but an international search had failed to locate the prophet. In the middle of this turmoil God arranged for His two key men to meet up. Obadiah was searching out pasture for Ahab's horses when he bumped into Elijah. A chance meeting? Nope!

GOD HAS EVERYTHING PLANNED.

>ENGAGE

The people we meet are God's appointments for us. We meet no one by chance. That's why it's good to ask God to help us make the best of the opportunities we have. When you meet other Christians, do all you can to encourage them. Some work quietly behind the scenes to serve God while others are more up front – but we all need to support each other.

SUPPORT

MAN OF HIS WORD

"'Haven't you heard, my lord, what I did while Jezebel was killing the prophets of the LORD? I hid a hundred of the LORD's prophets in two caves, fifty in each, and supplied them with food and water. And now you tell me to go to my master and say, 'Elijah is here.' He will kill me!" Elijah said, "As the LORD Almighty lives, whom I serve, I will surely present myself to Ahab today.'" **1 Kings 18:13–15**

Obadiah had a problem. Elijah wanted him to set up a meeting between him and Ahab. Would it blow his cover? Would Elijah turn up at the meeting anyway?

IT WAS A TRICKY SITUATION. Ahab's police squad and Interpol had failed to find Elijah. If Obadiah reported his sighting it might look as if he had known where Elijah was all the time. He was hiding 100 prophets as it was. Obadiah was also concerned that God might beam Elijah to a new hiding place before the meeting. He would be for the *CHOP* if that happened.

Elijah promised he would turn up for a meeting that day. Could Obadiah trust him?

The answer was yes.

Obadiah had worshipped God from his youth and when Elijah promised in God's name to keep his word, he knew the prophet would face up to Ahab.

Both men were prepared to risk their lives to set up the next part of God's plan. Not only did they have to trust God but also each other.

Promises are only as dependable as the people who make them. Are you someone whom others can trust? One thing you can give and still keep is your word.

>ENGAGE

God makes promises but He has never had to make an excuse. Whatever He says – He does. Elijah kept his word and didn't let Obadiah down. God wants you to become a person who others can rely on. Broken promises cannot be mended, so it's important to keep your word.

WORD

TIPPING THE SCALES

"'I have not made trouble for Israel," Elijah replied. "But you and your father's family have. You have abandoned the LORD's commands and have followed the Baals. Now summon the people from all over Israel to meet me on Mount Carmel. And bring the four hundred and fifty prophets of Baal and the four hundred prophets of Asherah, who eat at Jezebel's table."' **1 Kings 18:18–19**

Things seemed very one sided at the weigh-in. Baal tipped the scales with the support of 850 priests and the sponsorship of Ahab and Jezebel. God only has the support of His second, Elijah, and zero sponsorship.

The animosity at the weigh-in was not pre-contest hype for the TV cameras either. Ahab accused Elijah of being a **TROUBLEMAKER.** Elijah jabbed a one-two about Ahab abandoning God's commands to dabble in the occult. The natural amphitheatre on Mount Carmel is an ideal location for the contest. The fight is expected to go the full distance.

We're caught up in an **EPIC STRUGGLE** between unseen forces of good and evil. It seems at times like it's a one-sided contest. Most people have little time for God and Christians seem to be in the minority. That didn't bother Elijah. He believed that 850 versus one wasn't unfair because God was on his side. More than that, he was prepared to speak up and let God act to show He is boss.

>ENGAGE

This is a great encouragement for times when people gang up to try and make us look foolish because we are Christians. Stand by God and He'll stand by you. His power can overcome any opposition.

PRAY

Father, thank You that You are always with me, standing by me. Help me to stand by You too. Amen.

THE FIGHT IS ON

'Elijah went before the people and said,
"How long will you waver between two
opinions? If the LORD is God, follow him;
but if Baal is God, follow him." But the
people said nothing.' **1 Kings 18:21**

Things are hotting up in the Big Fight press room.
The contest has national coverage and the 850 prophets
have been posing in their robes.

Attention now turns to the solitary figure of Elijah in his
camel skin kit, who makes a plea to the audience.

'It's make your mind up time, folks.' The ordinary
Israelites were undecided. Should they trust God or
do the expected thing and grovel to Baal? Many in the
crowd had reservations about Baal 'cos if he was the
'raining' champion, why hadn't he sent rain for three and
a half years? But **NO ONE DARED EXPRESS
THEIR DOUBTS,** or side with Elijah. Faced with
850 evil priests they played safe, kept quiet and awaited
the outcome of the contest before taking sides.

Elijah explained the rules of the contest. Both
sides would build an altar then pray. The god who
ANSWERED BY FIRE would be all powerful.
Whoever went first would have the advantage of the hot
midday sun overhead. But such is Elijah's trust in God that
he doesn't toss a coin. He lets Baal go first.

What a contrast between Elijah's faith, the faith of the people and the faith of the prophets of Baal. The prophets believed but pinned their hopes on a powerless god. The people wouldn't believe unless they saw evidence of God's power. Elijah simply trusted that God is who He says He is and waited for Him to act.

>ENGAGE

We can't please God without faith. God wants us to have the confidence to believe that He is who He says He is. We can only become Christians by believing that Jesus has the power to forgive our sins and make us holy. It's tempting at times to sit back and hope, rather than pray and let God show His great power. Talk with God about the struggles you face and ask Him to get involved to sort things out.

PRAY

Father, You understand my problems. Please help me to overcome them. Amen.

NO CONTEST

'Then the fire of the LORD fell and burned up the sacrifice, the wood, the stones and the soil, and also licked up the water in the trench. When all the people saw this, they fell prostrate and cried, "The LORD – he is God! The LORD – he is God!"'

1 Kings 18:38–39

The prophets of Baal float like a butterfly and sting like a bee. They're fired up, but that's about all!

It wasn't that Baal didn't have power. He may have been a bull-styled lump of stone but his image was a front for Satan worship. Satan was on show in the ring. No matter how much the prophets of Baal urged him on, he couldn't produce so much as a spark. God rendered him powerless. Elijah stood in God's corner, mocking his opponent: 'Shout louder! Maybe Baal has overslept ... or he's on holiday.'

It wasn't until the sun was setting that Elijah built his altar in the name of the Lord. He then soaked it with several gallons of water and prayed. God stopped sparring and went on the attack. A fireball fell from the sky, incinerating the sacrifice, the altar, stones and water. It was an *AWESOME KNOCKOUT PUNCH.*

The audience were left in no doubt who was the winner. The Lord (Yahweh) is God – **NO CONTEST!**

>ENGAGE

Elijah's faith was in the power of God's name. He built an altar in God's name and prayed in God's name. God's name is still as powerful today, as is the name of Jesus. At the name of Jesus, Satan and his evil forces do a runner, they are powerless to do otherwise. We are rescued from the punishment of our disobedience in the name of Jesus. Don't battle on against the odds when you can pray in God's name and have His help.

PRAY

Lord, You are God! No one else can stand up against Your power. Thank You for being my God too. Amen.

RESCUED

ON THE HORIZON

'Elijah said to Ahab, "Go, eat and drink, for there is the sound of a heavy rain." So Ahab went off to eat and drink, but Elijah climbed to the top of Carmel, bent down to the ground and put his face between his knees. "Go and look toward the sea," he told his servant. And he went up and looked. "There is nothing there," he said. Seven times Elijah said, "Go back."'

1 Kings 18: 41–43

God is the **UNDISPUTED CHAMPION** of Israel! For three and a half years while the nation had been worshipping the rain god, it hadn't rained. God had stopped the rain and dew while Baal was being honoured. Now that the Israelites had quit looking for Baal to bale them out, God told Elijah He would switch on the water supply.

Elijah attended a summit meeting with God, praying for rain. Despite praying for a long time there wasn't any evidence that God was going to send rain. Elijah's servant kept looking, but as the hours passed there wasn't a cloud in the sky. Six times he reported that God hadn't answered Elijah's prayer. Did Elijah give up?

No, **HE KEPT PRAYING.** And the seventh time he prayed there was a rain cloud on the horizon!

Ahab packed up and drove his chariot off the floodplains. But he was overtaken by Elijah, powered by God, hotfooting it on a full marathon run – probably the fastest marathon in world history. Whether he was praying or cross-country running, Elijah never gave up.

>ENGAGE

When we don't get instant answers to our prayers it's tempting to stop talking to God. However, unless God has said no to our requests, we need to keep praying. When Jesus said, 'Ask and it shall be given to you', the meaning is 'ask and keep asking'. Don't think that prayer is battering on the gates of heaven to get our own way. Often God uses prayer to teach us how to fall in line with His plans.
If the request is wrong – God says no!
If the timing is wrong – God says slow!
If you are wrong – God says grow!
But if the request is right, the timing is right and you are right – God says go!

RISE UP SAMSON
VOW FOR LIFE

'Again the Israelites did evil in the eyes of the LORD, so the LORD delivered them into the hands of the Philistines for forty years. A certain man ... from the clan of the Danites, had a wife who was childless, unable to give birth. The angel of the LORD appeared to her and said ... "You will become pregnant and have a son whose head is never to be touched by a razor because the boy is to be a Nazirite, dedicated to God from the womb. He will take the lead in delivering Israel from the hands of the Philistines."' **Judges 13:1–3,5**

The Israelites returned to their selfish ways and it cost them their freedom for forty whole years. Their rulers, the Philistines, were big, muscle-bound iron men. As always, God had a rescue plan – this time in the beefy shape of Samson. Samson was born and bred as one of God's judges. His birth was announced by an angel with instructions that he was to live his life in total dedication to God by taking the Nazarite vow.

Whoever took the Nazarite vow was **FORBIDDEN TO CUT THEIR HAIR OR SHAVE THEIR BEARD.** Neither could they **DRINK ALCOHOL OR TOUCH A DEAD PERSON.** This vow was usually taken for thirty days. Samson's vow was for life. If a Nazarite deliberately broke his solemn promise he had to shave his head, bury the hair and start his vow all over again.

God needed a man who could say 'no' to temptation and 'yes' to Him. As Samson grew up there was no doubting he was a tough nut who could knock his opponents inside out.

>ENGAGE

To be able to say 'no' to temptation and 'yes' to God, you need the help of God's Holy Spirit. Talk with God about any problem areas where you feel compelled to go your own way rather than God's. Ask God to fill you with the Holy Spirit and make you alert to His warnings when you are heading towards trouble.

LION DOWN

'Samson went down to Timnah and saw there a young Philistine woman. When he returned, he said to his father and mother, "I have seen a Philistine woman in Timnah; now get her for me as my wife."' **Judges 14:1–2**

Samson never had a haircut as he grew up – impressive obedience in a hot country without shampoo, conditioner and gel, but can he resist temptation when it takes more shapely forms?

Samson knew that God had forbidden His people to marry idol-worshipping foreigners. But when he took a fancy to an attractive Philistine girl at Timnah, he didn't want to know God's views on the matter. Neither was he prepared to take his parents' advice. However, God was going to use Samson's *ARROGANCE* as a chance to disrupt the Philistines. On his way to his first date, Samson had a passionless embrace with a lion. Using his God-given superhuman strength, he shredded the beast with his *BARE HANDS.* He then set about chatting up the local Philistine beauty and became her 'mane man'. After a three-day whirlwind romance he proposed. What are the chances of this marriage working?

Samson's parents knew that God had commanded that there should be no marriages with people who served other gods, because it would drag God's people away from Him. By kicking against this, Samson was basically saying, 'I don't care that much about following God.'

>ENGAGE

It's not necessarily that God didn't want Samson to have a partner, but just not this one. God always wants the best for us. Sometimes the thing we want most is not what's best for us in God's eyes, and that can be hard to take. The question is: do we trust God enough to let go of that thing and believe that He will give us something better? How about you? Think about it: what do you need to talk to God about? What advice are you trying to ignore? Pray about it.

PRAY

RIDDLE ME THIS

'"Let me tell you a riddle," Samson said to them. "If you can give me the answer within the seven days of the feast, I will give you thirty linen garments and thirty sets of clothes. If you can't tell me the answer, you must give me thirty linen garments and thirty sets of clothes." "Tell us your riddle," they said. "Let's hear it." He replied, "Out of the eater, something to eat; out of the strong, something sweet." For three days they could not give the answer.' **Judges 14:12–14**

When Tate and Lyle were planning how to market their golden syrup, they illustrated an incident in Samson's life. This picture is still on their tins today, along with the answer to the riddle found in our Bible reading. **CHECK IT OUT** at the check out.

The vow of dedication to God that Samson had taken forbade him to touch any dead creature. But on passing the lion he had mauled three days before, he noticed a beehive inside its carcass and scooped out the honey. He was in a very sticky situation, not only planning to marry someone who worshipped idols but also breaking his promise to God.

His riddle exposed a side of his future wife's character

he had not seen before. The sweet girl from Timnah showed her claws, sulked, and made a scene to get her own way. Worse still, she **BETRAYED HIS TRUST** by telling her friends the answer to the riddle. Samson, scorching with anger at her disloyalty, buzzed off before the honeymoon. Rather than cancel the reception, the beauty from Timnah married Samson's best man instead. If only Samson had obeyed God and listened to his parents …

 >ENGAGE

Samson didn't care about letting God down but was very upset when the beauty from Timnah let him down. Think about your relationships and friendships. Have you ever felt you've been let down or that you've messed up? Pray for any situations you're in and also take a practical step to make amends.

DEDICATION

SUPERHUMAN RISE UP SAMSON

'Finding a fresh jawbone of a donkey, he grabbed it and struck down a thousand men. Then Samson said, "With a donkey's jawbone I have made donkeys of them. With a donkey's jawbone I have killed a thousand men."' **Judges 15:15–16**

Samson was more than a bit upset to find that his wife had run off with his best man, so he set fire to the Philistine crops and fruit. This made the Philistines burn with rage, so they set out to get Samson.

Samson kept up his tough man image, but inside **HE WAS DEEPLY HURT AND INSULTED**. To add to his betrayal, his fellow Israelites were prepared to hand him over to the Philistines to save their skins.

God was not going to let the idol-worshipping Philistines humiliate Samson anymore. Although Samson had let God down, **GOD WAS NOT GOING TO LET SAMSON DOWN.** He broke the ropes that bound Samson, then gave him the superhuman strength to get his teeth (or should that be donkey's teeth?) into the Philistines – all 1,000 of them!

Anger and hurt can easily wind us up. We can become so tied up with feelings of bitterness that God gets squeezed out of our lives. So remember that God will never let you down. He has the power to free you from any guilt, fear or anger that entangles your life. God gets alongside you when you need Him most to fight overwhelming problems. It's time to get your jawbone into action and talk with God about any matters you would like Him to get His teeth into.

PRAY

Father, thank You again that You never let me down and I can talk to You about anything that's on my mind. Amen.

FREE

HAIR TODAY, GONE TOMORROW

'Some time later, he fell in love with ... Delilah. The rulers of the Philistines went to her and said, "See if you can lure him into showing you the secret of his great strength ..." ... With such nagging she prodded him day after day until he was sick to death of it. So he told her everything ... After putting him to sleep on her lap, she called for someone to shave off the seven braids of his hair, and so began to subdue him. And his strength left him. Then she called, "Samson, the Philistines are upon you!" He awoke from his sleep and thought, "I'll go out as before and shake myself free." But he did not know that the LORD had left him.' **Judges 16:4–5, 16–17, 19–20**

Samson was a brave leader of the Israelites with a weakness for Philistine women. Being emotionally involved with the enemy became a way of life for him. At the time it may have seemed a really macho thing to do, adding to his reputation as being *ONE OF THE LADS,* but he was making a *BIG MISTAKE* as far as God was concerned.

Samson had vowed to put **GOD FIRST** all his life and his long hair was a symbol of that commitment. But when it came to a straight choice between obeying God or partying with Delilah, he chose to let his hair down.

Somehow Samson thought his secret sex life would not affect his relationship with God. But when he woke up as a skinhead his God-given superhuman strength was gone.

If only he had controlled his eyes and not been blinded by Delilah's deceptive charms … but by the time he could see how foolish he had been he could not see at all (16:21).

>ENGAGE There are many ungodly things in life that tempt us and this is not made easier by people, sometimes the majority, saying: 'It's OK, everyone's doing it.' Don't be blind to what God says is sin. He wants to spare you the damaging consequences these things can bring to your life. Why not explore the theme of temptation with some of your Christian friends? Find some Bible verses that help us understand what temptation is and how we can deal with it.

CRUSHED

'Then Samson prayed to the LORD, "Sovereign LORD, remember me. Please, God, strengthen me just once more, and let me with one blow get revenge on the Philistines for my two eyes." Then Samson reached towards the two central pillars on which the temple stood. Bracing himself against them, his right hand on the one and his left hand on the other, Samson said, "Let me die with the Philistines!" Then he pushed with all his might, and down came the temple on the rulers and all the people in it. Thus he killed many more when he died than while he lived.' **Judges 16:28–30**

Without God's strength Samson was a wimp. But God didn't desert the wayward superhero. Samson's last hair-raising act was to *BRING THE HOUSE DOWN.*

Samson's hair was a symbol of his commitment to God. When he disobeyed the Lord he lost his hair, eyesight, freedom and strength. As he trod the mill as a prisoner of the Philistines, he realised how foolish he had been and rededicated his life to God. When he was ridiculed in the heathen temple he spoke to God as his Sovereign Lord.

Finally, he **LEARNT THE HARD WAY** that God was in charge and God knew best.

As Samson's recommitment to God grew, so did his hair. The Philistines thought Samson was a pushover. And in a strange kind of way he was. As he experienced God's power in his life again, he pushed over the temple supports. It was a crushing victory.

>ENGAGE

When we seriously head away from God, He never writes us off. When we truly regret our disobedience and meet God on His terms, our relationship is restored. Not only are we forgiven but God also wants to use us to achieve great things for Him. There is never any ceiling to what you can do for God, providing you ask for His strength. Ask God to give you the strength you need to live today for Him.

DAN LIONHEART 02
LAST ORDERS

'He did this because Daniel, whom the king called Belteshazzar, was found to have a keen mind and knowledge and understanding, and also the ability to interpret dreams, explain riddles and solve difficult problems. Call for Daniel, and he will tell you what the writing means.'

Daniel 5:12

We rejoin Daniel's story as Belshazzar takes over from his dad, King Neb. Belshazzar had no time whatsoever for God. *HIS PARTIES WERE WILD.* And none were wilder than the one where he and his mates got totally drunk drinking out of goblets that had been taken from the Temple in Jerusalem. Enough was enough. *GOD CALLED LAST ORDERS.*

The party sobered to a standstill as a floating hand traced some mysterious words in the plaster on the wall. Belshazzar went pale, got the shakes and collapsed. You don't mock God and get away with it.

He became a quivering wreck with that 'mourning'-after-the-night-before feeling. And none of his Babylonian wise guys could help him.

The queen knew the only man in the kingdom who could explain the mysterious words – this was a job for Dan.

A pale-faced Belshazzar sent out an SOS to Daniel. Dan had been sidelined by the new king but his reputation as a wise and holy man lived on. God was about to bring His superhero out of retirement.

Notice that Daniel wasn't at this party.

Maybe he wasn't invited but you can be sure that if he'd received an invitation he'd have probably declined. Parties where you feel uncomfortable are best avoided. This one deteriorated into a free-for-all where God was openly ridiculed. Daniel might have been thought of as a bit of a square on the party scene but people respected him for his wisdom and his faith. And in a moment of crisis he was available to be used by God.

 Are you on call for God today? Keep in touch with Him and be ready for action.

ERROR OF THEIR WAYS

'You praised the gods of silver and gold, of bronze, iron, wood and stone, which cannot see or hear or understand. But you did not honour the God who holds in his hand your life and all your ways. Therefore he sent the hand that wrote the inscription.' **Daniel 5:23–24**

Dan dared to refuse the king's offer of a reward for explaining the mysterious words in the plaster. You don't turn down the offer of a purple robe lightly, that was the ultimate in designer clothes. Neither do you easily turn down the offer of a gold chain and promotion to third in the kingdom. But Daniel was there as a prophet, not to make a profit.

Dan also dared to give the king a brief review of the error of his ways. Basically Belshazzar hadn't learnt the *HARD LESSONS* God had taught his father Neb. The king had remained arrogant and proud, *REFUSING TO CREDIT THE MOST HIGH GOD* for giving him power.

Dan then dared to point out the serious issue of blaspheming God's name and getting drunk while boozing from the Temple goblets. Belshazzar squirmed. He'd acted all big and tough in front of his mates but it wasn't funny anymore.

Dan was now daring to reveal the meaning of the mysterious writings. He humbly spoke the words God had given him. The subdued king listened quietly, without protest.

Meanwhile, just outside the city walls, King Darius and his Persian army were looking for a way into the heavily defended city of Babylon. It was impossible to break through the walls, but by diverting the river they could crawl into the city along the dried-up river bed.

>ENGAGE

It's important we don't get 'holier than thou' with people, especially when we're explaining the need for God's forgiveness. People will listen if they think we're genuine and not putting one over them. Ask God to help you to be patient in a tight situation.

PRAY

Lord, You are always patient. Help me to be patient with people too. Amen.

ON THE SCALES

'God has numbered the days of your reign and brought it to an end ... You have been weighed on the scales and found wanting ... Your kingdom is divided and given to the Medes and Persians.'

Daniel 5:26–28

Dan dared to tell the badly shaken king the meaning of the words God had written in the plaster. Even as he spoke, unknown to them both, the Medes and the Persians were making their way into the city up the dried-up river bed.

The news wasn't good for Belshazzar. His days as a selfish so-and-so were over. He'd *TIPPED GOD'S SCALES* as grossly overweight with pride and rebellion. His kingdom would be captured by the Medes and the Persians.

When God puts us on the scales and our good deeds outweigh our bad deeds, are we OK? Just one nanogram of disobedience tips the balance against us. It's just not possible to work our way into God's good books. *THAT'S WHY WE ASK JESUS TO FORGIVE US.* Only Jesus can tip the balance in our favour.

When God speaks about judgment, He means it. No sooner had Belshazzar honoured Daniel than the Medes and Persians infiltrated the palace. That night the bad Babylonian king became history and the Medes and Persians took control of his empire.

Daniel's life was spared. God had more daring escapades planned for him. He honours those who honour Him! Now, where have you heard that before?

>ENGAGE

Proud Belshazzar acted big, mocked God in front of his mates and mistreated people. When he realised the error of his ways it was too late. Are you making the most of the opportunities you have to put your life right with God? Sometimes we need to be reminded that a future without God is hell – but a future with God is heaven. Don't put God on hold if He has been trying to get your attention. His warnings may be tough to take but they're always for our good.

INCORRUPTIBLE

'They could find no corruption in him, because he was trustworthy and neither corrupt nor negligent. Finally these men said, "We will never find any basis for charges against this man Daniel unless it has something to do with the law of his God."' **Daniel 6:4–5**

Darius, the new king on the block, appointed Daniel as one of his three deputies in charge of the money coming in from 120 provinces. This was a top job and one of the perks was being able to fiddle the books to line your own pockets. **EVERYONE WAS DOING IT.** Tax collectors overcharged and pocketed the difference. Daniel dared to be different.

Other yuppies, jealous of such a top job going to a Jew, decided to discredit Daniel and went digging for dirt. They swooped like a pack of Sunday newspaper journalists, interviewing his neighbours, ransacking his rubbish sacks and setting him up. But Daniel emerged as a decent, honest guy.

So they went through his accounts with a fine-tooth comb. He must be on the take, everyone else was. To their amazement, and disappointment, Daniel's accounts were in order. There wasn't a hint of any bungs, fixes, dodgy handshakes or secret Swiss bank accounts. Dan dared to be honest.

So the rat pack decided to set Daniel up to disobey the king. They knew that Daniel openly prayed three times a day facing Jerusalem – **WITHOUT FAIL.** By setting up a month of Darius-only worship they had Daniel trapped.

>ENGAGE

Some people think it's smart to cheat or fiddle the books. Some think it's OK to shoplift or deceive. That's not God's way. Daniel dared to be honest. There were no shifty shekels in his pockets. Our God is a God of truth – He is absolutely honest. And when we play it straight we honour God. So if you're still running a few dodgy deals, settle the matter with God and with those who have unfairly lost out. Honesty is a great way to bring credit to God.

'Now when Daniel learned that the decree had been published, he went home to his upstairs room where the windows opened towards Jerusalem. Three times a day he got down on his knees and prayed, giving thanks to his God, just as he had done before.'

Daniel 6:10

When Daniel knew he'd been **SET UP** he could've kept a **LOW PROFILE** for thirty days. As long as he didn't pray facing Jerusalem no one would know he wasn't worshipping the king. But Daniel dared to keep up his habit of praying three times a day, with his windows open – facing Jerusalem. Why did Dan risk becoming lion luncheon meat?

There was a vital reason why Daniel didn't bow.

God had told the Jews that while they were captives abroad, if they prayed facing Jerusalem He would answer their prayers and bring them back to their land. They would also be able to rebuild the Temple in Jerusalem!

Daniel knew he must dare to keep praying. It was their **ONLY HOPE** of being able to worship God in Jerusalem again. Not only did he pray but also he gave thanks as he prayed. Could you have given thanks knowing you were putting yourself on the lions' menu?

Dan knew the important thing was to stay in touch with God – at all costs.

Historical Note:

In the second year of King Darius, the Jews were given permission to rebuild the Temple in Jerusalem. It took them six years to finish the project. What caused the king to make this decision? We don't know, but Daniel's prayers must have played a part.

>ENGAGE

Daniel wouldn't miss his prayer times for anything. His habit of prayer not only made a difference to his life but to the future of the nation! Do you really believe that talking with God makes a difference? Talk with some of your Christian firends about how God has answered prayer. Encourage each other to make and keep a habit of daily prayer.

THE LIVING GOD

'I issue a decree that in every part of my kingdom people must fear and reverence the God of Daniel. For he is the living God and he endures for ever; his kingdom will not be destroyed, his dominion will never end. He rescues and he saves; he performs signs and wonders in heaven and on earth. He has rescued Daniel from the power of the lions.'

Daniel 6:26–27

The law of the Medes and the Persians couldn't be changed. Darius reluctantly sealed Dan *INTO THE LIONS' DEN.* 'May your God, whom you serve continually, rescue you,' said Darius, and he meant it. The king had *GREAT RESPECT* for Dan – the man who refused to stop worshipping his God.

The king's conscience was troubled by the whole setup. But he was the only one who had anything to chew over that night. Although the lions were starving hungry (just look at the way they downed the alternative menu in verse 24), God stopped them getting their claws on Dan.

Before knowing that Daniel was still alive, Darius was addressing God as the 'living God'. And when Daniel emerged without a scratch, Darius gave God **ALL THE PRAISE.** The king even wrote to all the 120 provinces in his kingdom telling them that the 'living God' saves and rescues.

Dan trusted God to save him and God did! God is still in the save and rescue business.

>ENGAGE

Do you feel trapped in a situation right now? Ask God for His help and He'll protect and lead you – just like He did for Daniel. The God who set Daniel free is the same God who can set you free too.

PRAY

Father God, thank You for always helping me, protecting me and leading me. Please help me to keep trusting You. Amen.

NOT GUILTY

'In my vision at night I looked, and there before me was one like a son of man, coming with the clouds of heaven. He approached the Ancient of Days and was led into his presence. He was given authority, glory and sovereign power; all nations and peoples of every language worshipped him.' **Daniel 7:13–14**

What was Dan dreaming about? He'd fast-forwarded in time to see events still to take place. But what did it all mean? He wasn't afraid to ask for help (7:16).

The code was cracked. The 'Ancient of Days' was God. The 'son of man' was not so easy for Dan to understand – 'God in human form'. Now we know who that is – Jesus!

Daniel was getting a preview of God *JUDGING THE WORLD.* The court was in session with God on the throne and the whole of mankind in the dock. The books were open and the charges about to be read. But who was this arriving in court? Jesus? And Jesus is being *HONOURED BY EVERYONE.* People from every nation are worshipping Him.

Now we shouldn't be surprised by this. Paul talks about this future scene too. He told the Christians in Philippi that 'at the name of Jesus every knee should bow, in heaven and on earth and under the earth, and every tongue acknowledge that Jesus Christ is Lord' (Phil. 2:10–11).

Such was the drama of the courtroom scene that Daniel went pale (7:28). Should we be troubled at the prospect of meeting up with Jesus in the future? Not if Jesus is your Saviour, because the verdict is 'not guilty' – He has paid the price of your forgiveness.

>ENGAGE

One day everyone will face Jesus either as their Saviour or their Judge. And there won't be any atheists in court. Everyone, no matter what they thought of Jesus in their lifetime, will bow and honour Him. So why wait? Spend some time praising Him now.

PRAY

Lord God, You are awesome! You are my Saviour and my King! I love You! Amen.

GOD HAD HEARD

'He instructed me and said to me, "Daniel, I have now come to give you insight and understanding. As soon as you began to pray, a word went out, which I have come to tell you, for you are highly esteemed."'

Daniel 9:22–23

When Dan was reading the Old Testament he suddenly realised there was some **GREAT NEWS** he hadn't seen before. He was reading from Jeremiah, a prophet who had been around when he was a young lad. Jeremiah had written down that Jerusalem would lie in ruins for seventy years. Dan did a quick calculation and realised that seventy years was nearly up. God must be planning to get the Jews back to Jerusalem soon.

So what did Dan do? He talked the matter through with God. This wasn't a casual chat though. Daniel concentrated all his effort and energy into pleading with God to deliver them (9:20). First he spent time confessing his sin and **GETTING RIGHT WITH GOD.** He was sorry and he meant it. Then he apologised to God for the disobedience of the Jews. Finally he asked God to bring the Jews back to Jerusalem – just as He had promised.

One evening as he prayed Dan saw a vision of the angel Gabriel. This was great news. God had heard his prayers, right from the first word he uttered. And what's more, God had answered them!

Dan dared to claim a promise of God. History records that a year later 42,000 Jews were back in Jerusalem rebuilding the Temple. And how long did the Temple lie in ruins? Exactly seventy years. Good or what?

>ENGAGE

Daniel made a life-changing discovery through reading the Bible. It encouraged him to devote more time and energy into prayer. As you read your Bible today, ask God to show you new things. Spend some time getting sorted out with God – because He's listening before you say your first word. He always keeps His promises and His timing is always right.

PRAY

God, even when I have finished reading this book, help me to make sure I still read Your Word every day. Amen.

THE GREAT WAR

'Do not be afraid, Daniel. Since the first day that you set your mind to gain understanding and to humble yourself before your God, your words were heard, and I have come in response to them.'

Daniel 10:12

Dan had been struggling for three weeks. Our superhero was on the rack. He kept praying to God but couldn't get any response. Why didn't God answer?

Daniel had had a **_MYSTERIOUS DREAM ABOUT A GREAT WAR,_** but he couldn't understand the details. He asked God to explain the dream but there was no reply. Silence followed by more silence.

Verse 13 gives us a clue as to what was happening behind the scenes. God had heard Dan's prayers from the very first word. But there was a mega battle going on between good and evil. The forces of evil were trying to block the heavenly forces. Satan is powerless to stop God from working, but that doesn't stop him trying to delay God's plans.

We need to realise that **PRAYER CAN SOMETIMES BE A STRUGGLE.** When we speak with God, there are evil forces who want to stop it becoming a serious conversation. They bring doubts that God is listening or willing to help you. And too often Christians give up and give in. Dan dared to keep praying even when he didn't get any answer. He dared to keep praying even though he felt so low.

>ENGAGE

Don't ever doubt that God hears your prayers. His answers may not be immediate, or the answers you wanted, but He will break through. So keep praying, especially when you don't feel like it. Be confident that God is working on your answer behind the scenes.

PRAY

Father, even if I am tired, bored, stressed or angry, please remind me that I can always pray to You, and You will always listen. Amen.

LAMB OF GOD

'everyone whose name is found written int he book – will be delivered ... Those who are wise will shine like the brightness of the heavens, and those who lead many to righteousness, like the stars for ever and ever. But you, Daniel, roll up and seal the words of the scroll until the time of the end. Many will go here and there to increase knowledge.' **Daniel 12:1,3–4**

Dan is fast-forwarded to the future again. Let's freeze-frame what he saw in his dream. Everyone **WHO HAS EVER LIVED** is about to be judged by God. A mysterious book is opened … There is bad news and good news. The bad news (very seriously bad news) is for those not written in the book. They are banished out of God's presence in shame. But there's good news (amazingly good news) for those listed in the book. They're given a 'not guilty' verdict and remain with God forever.

So what's this book? And who's in it? The book lists all those booked into heaven. Check out Revelation 21:22–27. It's called the 'Lamb's book of life'. So who's the Lamb? That's a title given to Jesus – the Lamb of God who **DIED TO TAKE AWAY OUR SIN.**

So how do you get your name in the book? Only Jesus can enter your name there. Those who are genuinely sorry for their disobedience and ask Jesus to forgive them are written into the book.

Check out Daniel 12:13. God told Dan that his name was listed in the book of life. When Dan died he would rise to get his place in heaven and be rewarded for the faithful way he had served God.

Dan dared to honour God. And yes … God honoured Dan again and again.

>ENGAGE

So has Jesus booked you into heaven? Thank Him if you know He has, or ask a leader at Church to help you if you're not sure. Dan describes those who tell others how to get their names into the Lamb's book of life as shining 'like the stars'. Hey, you can be a star! As a young person, Dan dared to honour God. And God is still looking for young people who will dare to stand up and stand out for Him.

RISE-UP GIDEON
GOD HONOURS

'The Israelites did evil in the eyes of the LORD, and for seven years he gave them into the hands of the Midianites ... the angel of the LORD appeared to Gideon, he said ... "Take the second bull from your father's herd, the one seven years old. Tear down your father's altar to Baal and cut down the Asherah pole beside it. Then build a proper kind of altar to the LORD your God on the top of this height."'

Judges 6:1, 12, 25–26

We return to our revolutionary ride through the book of Judges with a look into the life of Gideon – one of the all time great judges.

In this section, the angel of the Lord comes to speak to Gideon and lets him know that the Lord is with him. Gideon is surprised because it seems that God has **LEFT ISRAEL FOR DEAD,** as it is occupied by the Midianites. He needs a bit of reassuring, so God barbecues his soup, meat and bread without using matches (or a barbecue!). The problem is always that Israel has **TURNED AWAY** from God to false gods. Gideon protests that surely God doesn't want to use a 'nobody' like him to rescue Israel, but God insists.

Obeying God sometimes makes life difficult. Poor Gideon faced a lynch mob the next morning. But God always honours those who honour Him. Gideon's father came to the rescue, telling the mob that Baal was big enough and ugly enough to fight his own battles. Baal never emerged from the rubble and God protected Gideon.

>ENGAGE

Before God can work powerfully in your life He needs to rule in your life. Think for a minute and maybe talk over with a Christian leader how we can come to worship people or things more than we worship God. What in your life might God want you to tear down so you can put Him first? What does God do for those who honour Him?

PRAY

Father, show me the things in my life I need to change so I can put You first. Amen.

Now allow God time to answer. Put aside time just to think about God.

TRUST HIM

'Gideon said to God, "If you will save Israel by my hand as you have promised – look, I will place a wool fleece on the threshing-floor. If there is dew only on the fleece and all the ground is dry, then I will know that you will save Israel by my hand, as you said." And that is what happened. Gideon rose early the next day; he squeezed the fleece and wrung out the dew – a bowlful of water.'

Judges 6:36–38

Gideon was always **DOUBTING HIS BELIEFS AND BELIEVING HIS DOUBTS.** He was a man who put question marks where God had put full stops.

Notice that God wrung out the dew, not the Jew who doubted He would give the Israelites victory over their powerful enemies. **GOD PATIENTLY REASSURED GIDEON** not once, but twice.

God is pleased when we trust Him, despite the things that Satan uses to try to undermine our faith. It is vital that you read the Bible regularly and talk over any doubts you have with God. Your faith toughens up when you hear God speak to you through the Bible. The more you get into your Bible the more confidence you will have in God.

When it comes to doing something where we have to rely totally on God for success, we too can feel a bit sheepish. But God is totally reliable. When He says He'll give you the power to do something, He means it. We can have all kinds of doubts at different times in our Christian lives. So we need to do what Gideon did and take our doubts to God. God knows that our trust in Him is shaky at times, but is pleased to reassure us that He is in control.

PRAY

Lord, help me get stuck into the Bible and put my trust in You. Amen.

CONTROL

OUTNUMBERED

'The LORD said to Gideon, "You have too many men. I cannot deliver Midian into their hands, or Israel would boast against me, 'My own strength has saved me.' Now announce to the army, 'Anyone who trembles with fear may turn back and leave Mount Gilead.'" So twenty-two thousand men left, while ten thousand remained. But the LORD said to Gideon, "There are still too many men."'

Judges 7:2–4

Gideon knew he had a fight on his hands. The mighty Midianites – over 120,000 of them – were camped, ready to raid Israel. He bravely mustered 32,000 men to head them off.

OUTNUMBERED 4–1 and God said Gideon had too many men. Why? God wanted Gideon to trust that He has the power to win no matter what the odds. So Gideon dismissed all those who hadn't got the bottle for a fight. There were 22,000 wimps who headed back to their mummies. Gideon's army was now outnumbered 12–1. Still far too many for God, who wanted to test just how much Gideon trusted Him.

So Gideon took his men for a drink and those who didn't remain on their feet were sent back to their tents. (They were only drinking water by the way!) Just 300 men were left – Gideon's army was now outnumbered 400–1. With these **RIDICULOUS ODDS,** God told Gideon He would give them victory. Would you have trusted God in the same situation?

>ENGAGE

Sometimes the odds look stacked against us. We want to do what God says but the situation looks impossible. It is when there is no clear way ahead and we are powerless to change the situation ourselves that our faith in God is tested. Gideon had only God's word that He would win the battle. But that was all he needed. When God promises something He carries it out, no matter what the odds.

PUTTING FAITH INTO PRACTICE

'During that night the LORD said to Gideon, "Get up, go down against the camp, because I am going to give it into your hands. If you are afraid to attack, go down to the camp with your servant Purah and listen to what they are saying. Afterwards, you will be encouraged to attack the camp."' **Judges 7:9–11**

Poor old Gideon. What chance do 300 men have against 120,000? God gives the order to attack … but He knew that Gideon needed more reassurance before he would make a kamikaze faith attack on the Midianites. So He arranged for Gideon to eavesdrop on the enemy.

Gideon discovered that God was already getting to the Midianites. One of them had dreamt of being steam-rolled by a bread roll. Did this mean they would end up as hamburger meat? Or be sandwiched by the Israelites? Whatever the meaning, the rumour spreading in the camp was that the God of the Israelites was going to **CRUSH THEM.** This was great news for Gideon. Yes, he could **TAKE GOD AT HIS WORD.**

God would give them victory. Gideon trusted God in theory but now he was prepared to put his faith into practice. His fears were gone and he took time out to worship God (see 7:15).

What a difference faith makes to our outlook on life. One minute Gideon is a nervous wreck, the next he is praising God for giving them victory before the battle. We don't need to wait to see God carry out His plans before we praise Him. If He says He will do something then give Him praise, because it is a dead cert He will. What can you praise Him for now?

Father, thank You for ...

... Amen.

A LOT OF NOISE

'Gideon and the hundred men with him reached the edge of the camp at the beginning of the middle watch, just after they had changed the guard. They blew their trumpets and broke the jars that were in their hands. The three companies blew the trumpets and smashed the jars. Grasping the torches in their left hands and holding in their right hands the trumpets they were to blow, they shouted, "A sword for the LORD and for Gideon!" While each man held his position round the camp, all the Midianites ran, srying out as they fled.'

Judges 7:19–21

Our roller-coaster revolution ride through the book of Judges reaches another high point. Three hundred Israelites on a night raid against the mighty Midianites.

Gideon bravely led his jazz band into battle. Never in the history of human conflict has so much been owed by so many, to so few trumpeters. On hearing the noise and seeing the hilltops covered in lights,

THE MIDIANITES PANICKED. What was coming to get them? A vast army? That giant bread roll? In the darkness they started attacking each other. Those who fled found their escape routes blocked by the Israelites. **GOD KEPT HIS PROMISE** and won another famous victory for the Israelites.

>ENGAGE

One person with God is an army! No matter what the odds, God is always a winner and those who team up with Him are winners too. You may not feel like a winner all the time, but our lives are part of a bigger picture that only God can see, and He knows the end. Praise God for the help He has given you in the past. Remember that He promises to be with you today.

PRAY

Father God, although I may not realise it all the time, thank You for not only always being on my team, but being the world's best team leader. Amen.

NEW GENERATION

'No sooner had Gideon died than the Israelites again prostituted themselves to the Baals. They set up Baal-Berith as their god and did not remember the LORD their God, who had rescued them from the hands of all their enemies on every side.' **Judges 8:33–34**

God helped Gideon to chase the Midianites out of Israel and bring them forty years of peace. A **NEW GENERATION** was growing up. Would they put their trust in the God who had helped their parents?

Frustratingly, no! As soon as Gideon was out of the way, the Israelites went shopping for something new to worship. Baal was a big hit with all the trendy nations around them. Half human, half bull, Baal was not a good-looking carved image, but he appeared to bring good harvests. So it seemed a good idea to 'Baal out' of obeying God and go along with this 'get rich quick', 'do your own thing' image. God had forbidden His people to make images of false gods or to worship them.

But the new generation of Israelites **DIDN'T CARE FOR GOD'S LAWS.** Neither did they want to obey their parents or show kindness to those who had helped them. Despite all Gideon had done for the nation, his family were left to fend for themselves.

>ENGAGE

Never forget to be kind to those who have helped you get to know God – parents, Sunday school teachers, youth leaders, experienced Christians. Thank God for the people who have helped you grow as a Christian. Are there any ways you can help and encourage them?

PRAY

God, thank You for all the awesome Christians in my life. Let them know how grateful I am for their guidance. Amen.

GUIDANCE

THE RESCUE

'In those days Israel had no king; everyone did as they saw fit.' **Judges 21:25**

Our revolutionary spin through the book of Judges is coming to an end. Just one verse to look at today – the last verse in the book.

The Israelites' roller-coaster ride stops at the lowest point. After all the thrills and spills of the many years when God has repeatedly rescued them, they are still doing their own thing.

God's laws are out. Living as you want, without a care for others, is in. It's a 'me first' not 'God first' society. Will they ever learn? Freedom is not living to please yourself, but *LIVING TO PLEASE GOD.* Are things different today? 'If it feels good – do it', has become a catchphrase for our modern way of thinking. And it is easy for us to get sucked into a spiral of selfish attitudes.

God was always there to *RESCUE* the Israelites and give them the *PEACE AND FREEDOM* they wanted. And God is always there to lift us up and set us right when we turn to Him. What a great, patient and loving God we have!

>ENGAGE What have you learnt from our long march through Judges? One thing we all need to guard against is becoming complacent and tracking downward in disobedience. Before we know it we will be diving into trouble. So talk to God regularly and read your Bible each day. Remember our ultimate revolutionary – Jesus Christ. Through Him we can always get back to our heavenly Father. If you know you are taking a dip in your Christian life, ask God to forgive you and fill you with the Holy Spirit. Praise Him for keeping His promises.

PRAY

Father God, keep my eyes fixed on You so that I'll always try to live to please You, not myself. Amen.

THE ELIJAH ESCAPE PLAN 02
UNCHANGING

'Elijah was afraid and ran for his life ... He came to a broom bush, sat down under it and prayed that he might die. "I have had enough, LORD," he said. "Take my life; I am no better than my ancestors." Then he lay down under the bush and fell asleep.' **1 Kings 19:3–5**

After such a **DRAMATIC VICTORY** you would think Elijah would be on a high. Instead he's on a downer – we're talking crash 'n' burn big time. His mountain top experience has evaporated into deep despair. What's gone wrong?

Elijah suddenly lost his bottle. When a furious Jezebel put him at the top of her hit list, the fearless prophet's knees were knocking. Instead of being bold for God, he did a runner, heading south out of the country. But why?

Elijah was human. Once the excitement of Mount Carmel was over, instead of taking time to talk through his next moves with God, he allowed himself to lapse into self-pity. The man who had looked up to God, looked down on himself.

Often when we experience God's power in our lives in some amazing way, we're brought down to earth afterwards with a bump. It's important that if we have achieved any success for God we turn to Him immediately for more strength, new challenges and direction. Try not to let your feelings lead you into thinking that God doesn't care about you. Our feelings may be up and down, but **GOD'S LOVE REMAINS THE SAME.**

>ENGAGE Just as we need fresh milk each day, we also need fresh inspiration from God. Yesterday's faith needs to be topped up today, which is why it is so important to read the Bible regularly and talk with God. Are you in an 'I've just about had enough' frame of mind? Don't run away. Talk it through with God ... Well, go on then!

RECHARGE

'The angel of the LORD came back a second time and touched him and said, "Get up and eat, for the journey is too much for you." So he got up and ate and drank. Strengthened by that food, he travelled for forty days and forty nights until he reached Horeb, the mountain of God.' **1 Kings 19:7–8**

Elijah has hit an all-time low. Physically he was exhausted, hungry and weak. Mentally he was convinced he was a failure. He didn't think he could be any more use to God. He collapsed, hoping to die.

Just look how gently God dealt with this deeply sensitive man. He sent an angel, not to tell him off but to feed him. The angel let him sleep before feeding him again. It wasn't in-depth counselling, just practical care and support. A **RESTED, REFRESHED AND MORE RELAXED** Elijah set off for Mount Horeb – the mountain where God had spoken to Moses. Whatever God had to say to Elijah could wait till he got there.

Focusing on our fears and failures can often lead to depression. Tiredness can also make us irritable or over-emotional. Sometimes a good night's sleep can do us a lot of good. It's God's way of refreshing our bodies and minds. It's great that God doesn't get heavy with us when we feel down. He's not looking to blame us but help us.

>ENGAGE

It's so easy to get eaten up with self-pity. It's so easy to get trapped into thinking you are a failure. That's why it's important to take time out to learn how much God values you. He cares for His children. Don't hold onto feelings of guilt or failure. Hand it over to God and move on.

PRAY

Lord, I want to hand my guilt and shame over to You. Help me see myself as You see me – as a valued son. Amen.

AFTER THE STORM

'After the earthquake came a fire, but the LORD was not in the fire. And after the fire came a gentle whisper. When Elijah heard it, he pulled his cloak over his face and went out and stood at the mouth of the cave.' **1 Kings 19:12–13**

When Moses had stood on Mount Horeb (also known as Sinai) God had spoken amid lightning, thunder, smoke and loud trumpet blasts. It was a laser and sound show that left the Israelites shaking with fear. Would God give Elijah the same treatment?

God let Elijah spill out all the concerns he had bottled up. He was still full of misery and self-pity. It wasn't fair … he was the only one left who worshipped God … his life was under threat … moan … mumble. God listened but didn't reply. Instead, He said He would pass by the mountain – just as He had done in the days of Moses.

There was an awesome multimedia display. Rocks shattered, the mountain shook, fire raged, but there was no sign of God. Then, in the quietness after the storm, **GOD SPOKE** in a gentle whisper. God knew Elijah was too frail to be shaken or blasted out of his self-pity. So He came gently alongside to coax Elijah into seeing things from a **DIFFERENT POINT OF VIEW.**

Self-pity gives us a distorted view of situations. Elijah thought he was out on a limb, the only person left who worshipped God. In reality there were 7,000 Israelites who were loyal to the Lord. Elijah thought his career as a prophet was finished. In reality, God still had important jobs for him to do. Elijah thought he would end up as a loner. In reality, God wanted Elijah to train up an assistant as his successor.

>ENGAGE

Sometimes we hold our fear and failures so close they're all we see. Situations can look so different from God's point of view. Elijah left Horeb when his circumstances hadn't changed, but he had. He now saw things from God's viewpoint, not his. The future was much better than he thought and he knew God really cared about him. God doesn't mind if we go on about our problems to Him. The important thing is to listen carefully for His reply.

PASSING ON THE MANTLE

'So Elijah went from there and found Elisha son of Shaphat. He was ploughing with twelve yoke of oxen, and he himself was driving the twelfth pair. Elijah went up to him and threw his cloak around him. Elisha then left his oxen and ran after Elijah.' **1 Kings 19:19–20**

When someone takes over someone else's job we sometimes use the expression 'he has taken on the mantle'. In Elisha's case that's exactly what he did.

God had told Elijah that Elisha, a young farming lad from the Jordan valley, was to be his apprentice and successor. Elisha (meaning 'God is salvation') was one of the 7,000 who were still loyal to God.

Elisha didn't apply for the job, it literally landed on him in the form of Elijah's mantle (cloak). Elijah's cloak was a symbol of God's power and authority, and when Elisha felt it on his shoulders he knew God had **CHOSEN HIM** to become a prophet.

Would he accept the job?

Being a prophet of God was a risky business when Jezebel was about – a dead-end job. Farming in the fertile Jordan valley had much better career prospects. However, Elisha knew that it's better to be where God wants you to be, doing what God wants you to do, than take the easy option. Showing his commitment to God he turned his plough into firewood and his valuable oxen into barbecue meat. There was **NO GOING BACK** now. He would have to rely on God for all his needs.

>ENGAGE

Elisha was prepared to learn how to serve God by tagging along as Elijah's trainee recruit. He learnt how to pray, worship and speak out for God. And he did so with the attitude of a servant. Do you realise that God has great plans for you? He's given you gifts and abilities that need to be developed.

PRAY

Father, thank You that You have great plans for me. Please help me to develop the abilities You've given me, and please put people around me who can help in this. Amen.

CONFRONTED

'the word of the LORD came to Elijah the Tishbite: "Go down to meet Ahab ... Say to him ... 'I am going to bring disaster on you. I will wipe out your descendants and cut off from Ahab every last male in Israel – slave or free ... because you have arounsed my anger'"' **1 Kings 21:17–19, 21**

King Ahab was close to **BREAKING POINT** after revelations that he and Jezebel murdered an innocent man to gain his land. Elijah claims that the two conspired to kill Naboth when he refused to sell a vineyard that Ahab wanted for a veggie garden. It was a plot about a plot.

Sources close to the king claim that he sulked in his bedroom when he couldn't get his way. Jezebel then framed Naboth for **A CRIME HE DIDN'T COMMIT** and had him executed. Attempts to hush up the incident were thwarted when God sent Elijah to confront Ahab and leak the news.

An ashen-faced Ahab looked shaken by God's claim that dogs would lick his blood in the same place they had licked the blood of the executed Naboth. Jezebel refused to comment on Elijah's prophecy that she would end up as a dog's dinner by the city wall at Jezreel.

Ahab was later killed by a stray arrow in battle. Dogs licked his blood off his chariot as it was washed at the well near where Naboth was murdered.

Ten years after Ahab's death, Jezebel was pushed to her death off the city wall of Jezreel.

>ENGAGE

You can fool some people all of the time, you can fool others some of the time, but you can't fool God. No one escapes the consequences of disobedience. Ahab's envy led to sulking, then murder. There is an 'I want ...' nature in all of us that can easily drive us off the right track. Greed affects our attitude to possessions and the way we treat people. It often results in others getting hurt.

PRAY

Lord, I don't want to be greedy or selfish. Please help me to be generous and honest, and show me when I'm treating people badly. Amen.

FIRED UP

'the angel of the LORD said to Elijah the Tishbite, "Go up and meet the messengers of the king of Samaria and ask them, 'Is it because there is no God in Israel that you are going off to consult Baal-Zebub, the god of Ekron?'"'

2 Kings 1:3

Elijah outlived his old sparring partner Ahab. Would Ahab's son Ahaziah learn from his father's mistakes and be a king who served God? Not a chance!

Ahaziah was the ultimate 'fall' guy. He fell out of a top storey window and was seriously injured. He fell for the lie that it was Baal and not God who knew what the future held. And he ultimately fell from power.

It was a case of like father, like son. Despite all the times God showed His power over Baal, Ahaziah grovelled to Baal-Zebul ('prince of Baal' – although the Bible purposely mispells it as Baal-Zebub which means 'lord of the flies').

Why was this such a serious mistake? Baal worship was nothing more than a front for Satan worship. So when Ahaziah snubbed God to consult Satan about his future, God moved in to show that He is in control of events.

Elijah was God's spokesman. He wasn't over the hill – as he once thought – but on top of it. And when two waves of fifty soldiers tried to bring him down, God fired them – literally. God, who had **ANSWERED WITH FIRE** on Mount Carmel in Ahab's day, answered with fire in Ahaziah's reign. His power is the same yesterday, today and forever.

Elijah, who had been burnt out for God, was now fired up for God – **HOLY SPIRIT FIRE** – ready to stand up and say that the New Age teaching of his time was seriously wrong. Consulting evil spirits about the future or asking them for healing is out of order.

>ENGAGE

There's no need to look anywhere but to God for anything. Talk with God, there's nothing He won't discuss with you.
The God who answers with fire wants to fire you up to live for Him today.

FIRE UP

SHOOTING THE MESSENGER

'The angel of the LORD said to Elijah, "Go down with him; do not be afraid of him." So Elijah got up and went down with him to the king.' **2 Kings 1:15**

What does Ahaziah do when he learns 100 of his crack troops have been caught in God's line of fire? Back down and bite his lip? No way. He stubbornly sends another fifty squaddies after Elijah.

Elijah stays put. He wasn't going to run away as he did when his life was threatened before. He knows God won't let him down. The third wave of soldiers are so scared of **GOD'S POWER** they hoist the white flag and want peace talks.

It's one thing to send a message that the king is wrong. It's another to tell him in person – which is what God wanted Elijah to do. Elijah went to the palace knowing he would make himself very unpopular (again!). What would the king want first, the bad news or the bad news?

He didn't **WATER DOWN** God's message either. He gave it to the king straight. Rejecting God has serious consequences. The king had refused to stand up for God – now he wouldn't be able to stand up for himself. He would be bedridden until he died.

>ENGAGE

Elijah was an upright man. Ahaziah was a downright fool. It's not easy to warn people who don't trust Jesus that they are making a serious mistake. Disobedience separates you from God forever. The great thing about the bad news is that there is so much good news to follow. Jesus is the answer! He's our one way back to God. Praise Him! Ask God to help you tell it like it is. Some will react like Ahaziah, reject the good news, ignore it or be really laid back. Others will want to know more. Talk with your leaders and friends at church about the things you have learnt from Elijah's exploits. How have his experiences helped you?

OVERFLOW

'Elijah said to Elisha, "Tell me, what can I
do for you before I am taken from you?"
"Let me inherit a double portion of your
spirit," Elisha replied.' **2 Kings 2:9**

For years, Elijah had been training Elisha, his second
in command, to take over as top gun when he'd gone.
Rumours were flying that the time to hand over was
approaching.

Jezebel had failed to destroy the prophets of God, and
Elijah helped set up schools to train new recruits. The
problem with trainee prophets is that you can't hide the
future from them. The prophets of Bethel told Elisha that
God was going to give Elijah a **FREE TRANSFER**
to heaven. So did the prophets at Jericho. But Elisha,
being a prophet, also knew that. Moses had disappeared
off by himself to be airlifted to heaven. Elisha wasn't
going to let Elijah do the same. He wanted to stay by
Elijah's side to see God act.

Years before, the power of God had stopped the River
Jordan flowing to let the Israelites into the promised
land. The same power, symbolised in Elijah's cloak,
made a path through the Jordan to let Elijah reach a new
promised land – heaven (see 2:8).

And what did Elisha hope to gain by staying close to Elijah? Everything and more! Elisha's greatest ambition in life was to be full of the Holy Spirit. He wanted a **DOUBLE HELPING!** Why? He wanted to make sure that God's Spirit wasn't just contained within him but **POURED OUT.**

>ENGAGE

There is nothing wrong in being ambitious for God. We are commanded to be full of the Holy Spirit, but there's nothing to stop us asking to be full to overflowing. God is generous with His power. We just need to ask Him to clean out our lives and we must be serious about keeping them clean.

PRAY

Lord, I want to be full to overflowing with Your Spirit. Please clean out my life, get rid of anything that's bad and help me follow You 100%. Amen.

AS GOOD AS HIS WORD

'Elisha then ... took the cloak that had fallen from Elijah and struck the water with it. "Where now is the LORD, the God of Elijah?" he asked. When he struck the water, it divided to the right and to the left, and he crossed over.' **2 Kings 2:13–14**

Elijah had seen God send **FIRE FROM HEAVEN** to win the contest on Mount Carmel, to protect him from his enemies and now to take him to heaven. As he talked with Elisha in the wilderness departure lounge, he suddenly took off. Elijah, the man who had been on fire for God, was fired up to be with God.

God didn't put the wind up Elisha. He kept his eyes open and his chin up to see the chariots of fire take off and climb in the air. It was the sign that God was going to give him the same power as Elijah and more. There was also another sign that **GOD HAD EMPOWERED ELISHA** to take over after the takeoff – Elijah had left his cloak in the departure lounge. Elisha took up the mantle at once, using it to slap open a path through the River Jordan as Elijah had done.

The other prophets were worried that Elijah might have crash-landed and sent out a search party. Elisha warned them they were wasting their time. God had never let Elijah down and He never would. When He promises a safe arrival in heaven, **HE MEANS IT.**

Elijah did get to heaven. There is more than God's word for it. Elijah was allowed to return to earth for a brief moment, along with Moses, to talk with Jesus on the Mount of Transfiguration. Peter, James and John saw Elijah with their own eyes and were totally stunned.

>ENGAGE

Not only has Jesus given us the chance for eternal life, but He's given us life in all its fullness now. Don't just wait in the departure lounge for heaven – ask God to fill your life with the Holy Spirit. From this moment on, your life can be a non-stop adventure, like Elijah's, as you share God's exciting life with others.

Prepare to grapple with some big questions!

Bold Brave Faith takes you through some of the most important topics central to our lives as guys today: teamwork, temptation, battles and struggles, and attitude. Just like *Stand Strong,* you can get stuck right in with Bible readings, Engage sections and prayers. Whether you have it by your bed, in your backpack or in your back pocket, it's a great tool for getting to grips with tough issues and God issues every day.
ISBN: 978-1-78259-099-6

Available from **www.cwr.org.uk/youth**

Also available online or from Christian bookshops

YP's daily devotional –
dig deeper into God's Word

Never did reading the Bible look so good! Get eye-opening, jaw-dropping Bible readings and notes every day, plus special features and articles in every issue (covers two months).

Available as individual issues or annual subscription. For current prices and to order visit

www.cwr.org.uk/youth

Also available online or from Christian bookshops

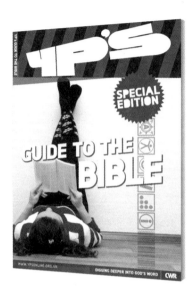

Get to know and understand the Bible

Written to help you know and understand the Bible
better, this exciting full-colour guide includes key
events, maps, timelines, major characters, explanations
of biblical terms and so much more!
ISBN: 978-1-85345-352-6

For current prices and to order visit
www.cwr.org.uk/youth

Also available online or from Christian bookshops